My Daily
Thoughts

CEDRIC EASTON

ISBN 979-8-88616-477-0 (paperback)
ISBN 979-8-88616-478-7 (digital)

Christian Faith Publishing
832 Park Avenue
Meadville, PA 16335
www.christianfaithpublishing.com

Printed in the United States of America

Anger

Anger is one of the strongest emotions. It comes out of heartache, pain, and frustration. It comes mostly from a place of unforgiveness for others as well as for ourselves. When anger introduces itself in a moment most of the time our action is on the ugly side, and we all know what comes after we blow up. So how do we counteract it? It is to not sin in our anger. When we sin in anger, it's like a wild fire within our bodies. Sin is the gasoline that accelerates the fire. It has a life of its own and will not back down or subside without help. We strongly have to let go and find the peace that passes all understanding. This is different from the anger Jesus had inside His Father's house. That was righteous anger. It also was a controlled fire in a direction which was not out of hatred but out of love and respect for His Father's house. Truth be told, that's the kind of anger we need in our humble hearts.

Anger is a way of life and so is sin because we are born into it. Let's do our best not to let them intertwine.

—Ephesians 4:31 (NIV)

Time of Peace

When asking for peace it can happen in an instant. But how do we accomplish it when in a rush? The peace that passes all understanding is not complicated when our mind is focused. We just have to envelop ourselves into a state of mind that is ready. We have to allow and trust God to handle what we can't. But most times that's not the first thing on our mind. So, let's take the time and think while saying a prayer. It's going to be okay! It can be said soft and quiet, or bold like a lion, a roaring crying out in the midst of a raging storm! From where Jesus started to where He said, "It's finished" there was peace. How much peace that passes all understanding was Jesus portraying in the midst of His crucifixion? What was going through His mind? I certainly don't think our pain can measure up to His but we have come close to it.

Cooler heads will prevail, but peace that's from
heaven warms the spirit.

—Philippians 4:7 (NKJV)

The Day of Words

Be mindful of today, of the words we say, because we can give life and take it away. We can make someone happy and put a smile on their face. Or we can turn it all the way around and speak hate. Into the place where love resonates (thumps of thumps), in every second of the day, we can speak life or take it away. We didn't realize sometimes the impact when as a child we made fun of others. Saying to someone they are looking bummy, not knowing what's going on in their life at home. But the real tragedy is when he or she grows up doing things and becoming someone who they weren't supposed to be. Even though God knows which road we will follow, still it's a very hard pill for a child to swallow. We can't fix the back then, but we can start talking to everyone as if they are our loved ones.

An insult thrown into a small or gaping wound will burn the flesh. An insult thrown into a fit of hot rage will seek out death in the hearts of those it touches. But if the wounds are treated with the word from out of heaven, the skin will be cool to the touch and life will dance in the hearts it lives in.

—Proverbs 15:1 (NKJV); Proverbs 17:5 (NIV)

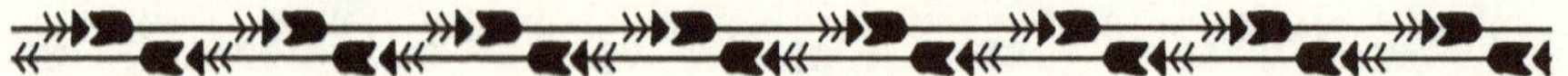

In Due Time

When it's time to put in work let us not hesitate in doing well. Some of us have wasted a lot of time waiting on the perfect time to do what God asked, not knowing that there's no such thing as our perfect timing in the work of God. God has a special way of handling His works that are in us and for us to do. We definitely cannot do anything on our own time or life will be short and difficult. We also cannot forget that it's not us, but it's the Holy Spirit who guides us and keeps us in the right time zone.

To allow God's timing to flourish deep
within us the timing will be perfect.

—Deuteronomy 32:4 (NIV)

Over Here or over There

The good is always around, and the bad and the ugly are not too far behind. Hate and fear are tight to the end of days. They are buddies trying to take down love. Yet love is bold, full of life. It cannot live in the same facility as those two brothers. It stands alone on either side, creating a line defined and it dares those against it. Love does not struggle or haggle; it doesn't duck nor dodge its way around. However, it does walk the fine line of truth and that cannot be escaped.

Putting love into anything takes the love out of the
things we ought to be putting love into.

—1 Corinthians 13:13 (NIV)

Part of Life

Forgiveness is a part of life. Verbally forgiving others for what was done to us brings comfort to the heart. It relaxes our spirit. Meanwhile it also puts the other at ease within their soul, and I am pretty sure it puts a big smile on God's face. We, as a people, really don't truly look at the significance of honesty in forgiving one another. We say the words in earnest, with a humble heart, and yet, we can't see the DNA that makes up the events that are going to unfold in that person's life or ours. As children of God that is the condition of life we live in, to forgive brothers, sisters, and those that are yet to come to the body of Christ Jesus.

> To forgive with a heart of God will encounter is a full life
> sentence. But whosoever does not forgive will encounter
> a long sentence without the possibility of life.
>
> —Matthew 6:15 (KJV)

The Day of the *Yes*!

The day of the *yes* is when we said to Jesus come into my life. When we say it as kids to please our parents we really don't understand what we've just done. But to recognize the significance of that as a young adult and to mean it as an adult is outstanding. Three things are going to happen throughout this magnificent journey of wisdom and understanding of a child of God. First is staying on the course of a godly life all the way until the end as best as we can. Second is when we fall just rededicating our lives back to God. And third is all hell will break loose when we die after a good time in this world. God has not forgotten that day of our *yes*! We, as His children, have gone through the good, the bad, and the downright ugly side of life. God is not going to make it hard for us, but evil is not going to be easy on us. Yet it will be bearable to live a righteous life.

Some will say, "Yes!" Some will say, "No!" Some
will just toss it in the air as the wind blows.

—Romans 14:11 (NKJV)

On This Day

Part One

We will have plenty of days like this. When we help someone out that's going to have a major impact on their lives. Love should always be the motivation to help another person out. But that's not always the case. Hidden agendas will be a factor in someone's heart. Most know what they are doing and yet others have no clue of what's happening in the background. Helping out of love is not an act nor is it a thought. The true act of love is God and His alone. God is not a puppet master pulling the strings. Except on the curtains to reveal what He has been in our lives. As we are helping each other God is helping us.

Don't worry! The helper always gets help!

—Galatians 6:1 (NIV)

My Day

Part Two

We know this very well. When there is no one around to talk to or call on for help at the moment. As we call on Father, the Son, or the Holy Spirit to come in our time of need. But sometimes when it gets so hectic, anxiety gets to kicking in, our arms start flying all over the place, and at the same time some are thinking. I'm always helping others out. How come there's no one here to help me? But we quickly realize that God is here in my day to keep me calm. In the midst of the storm, to restore me back to patience and to remind me that He's always will be with me.

Help is coming, and it's not just a matter of time.

—Psalm 30:10 (NKJV)

Entering the Day

As the day starts, we do our regular routine expecting everything to go the way it should. No matter what kind of bumps are in the middle of the road. We know as children of God "that this is the day He has made." So, we have to expect. The things to go God's way especially when we start the day off with Him. We do get sidetracked from time to time. But we don't allow ourselves to go off the rails and handle things on our own. God is the day maker, and He's the difference-maker as well. We don't have to define our day because it's already been defined for us. The only thing we have to do is rejoice and be glad in it.

The time and the place has been set. We just have to be ready!

—Psalm 91:4 (NKJV)

Step Back into That Day

The things we have done to others and the things that have been done to us. It's all in the past. We can no longer allow ourselves to be an instrument of discord. Some of us have mishandled some past situations in an ungodly manner and went to bed on it within our hearts. Knowing that's not of us to do so as children of God. In moments like this, we have to take steps back and look at what got us to this point. So we can ask forgiveness from both parties and allow the Holy Spirit to make way for righteous moments to come. We all know when the day comes. When the talk of saying I'm sorry to another child of God is more enjoyable to God than to us.

When we take steps back into hurt to heal the pain
we've caused can only strengthen us in one way…

—Psalm 19:9 (NIV)

Step into Another Day

Our mind is something to behold. It has so many marvelous things that come from it and yet so much tragedy has plagued it. Some memories keep us from moving on and out of the stagnant waters. Some like myself (Cedric Easton) take trips off into no man's land only to return with a fake smile and joy that does not please the Father. But as for today, our minds are being renewed in a major way. With an overhauled into righteousness being stored in all the corners of the mind. Our step back into our memories and actions that were not of God is not an option that we can indulge in. Our memories may cause us some kind of turmoil and a psychedelic trip into the past. But we cannot forget all that God has done in our past in the midst of the bad and the ugliness. Our past is not in discomfort. It's a blessing.

> The only time we take a step back is to reflect on what
> God has done in our lives. Also, to teach ourselves what
> not to do or from doing it in a different way because
> that is just a plan. Insanity! And God doesn't deal with
> insanity. That is why there are patted rooms in heaven.

> —Romans 12:2 (NIV)

The Way of the Day

In many ways, most days start off well without care and are harmless in nature. We tell ourselves that God got this day in His hands. With the world evils throwing a fit and trying to get their job done for the day. There are some days when it gets really jumbled up some lose control. We all have been tangled up in the day of days. Especially when some of us are used to letting go and letting chaos consume our thoughts and action. Meanwhile others jump out of the hands of God in the grips of their own lives. But that does not mean that God is not going to help us through this. Even the ones who think they don't deserve it. God has a plan for all the actions we've taken through our struggles. The only ways our day can make it good, bad, or downright ugly. It all depends on who we let control the day.

Out of three pairs of hands. There's only one that works.

—Matthew 6:25 (NIV)

Just for the Day

To be strong enough to take hold of the strongholds in life and give them on to God. Many of us have strongholds; they are tough enough individually. But when they get together they have a life of their own. We cannot fight them on our own, and we know this. But it's hard for some to truly ask God to give them the strength to be overcome. It's a worldwide thought that comes down to the same conclusion. We do not know what the next person is going through. Anything that comes to our mind is impossible to imagine. In another person's life that they are dealing with. That is why we ask God for enough strength just for today.

Don't get upset when everything has been done with the strength that has been given. There are no take-backs, but there will always be what-ifs and only God can fix that.

—Matthew 6:27 (NIV)

The Day of New

There's nothing new under the sun, and yet our future has not been made until the moment arrives. Even though God knows what's going to happen, it's still new to us. The newness that happens is not just in the things that we experience that are new that's even in our daily routine. Things that we do on the regular are still new and not just because it's a new day either. When Jesus was here in His flesh, He performed miracles, and He said that we will do greater things than He. Even though things have been done on this earth by others. It does not mean that our love, kindness, gentleness, patience, and self-control are old. It's just a new kind of old.

Our sight is new. The words we say are new, and the breath
we breathed in is new. The life we live is new. Even when
we look back on the old, it is because we are new.

—2 Corinthians 5:17 (NIV)

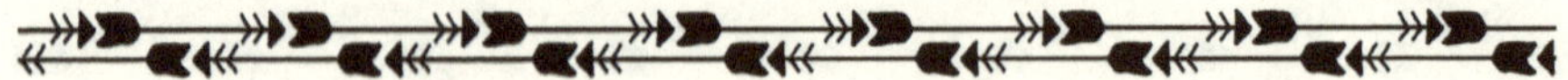

The Day within the Day

The things that happen at the moment sometimes are not seen clearly. And if we are not seeing clearly our mind isn't either. Our actions get thrown all out of weakness. Like a child that doesn't understand the word no or an animal in a fit of rage. Most of us have been there in and out of the Holy Spirit. Even though we've apologized to our brothers and sisters. But most of all it's really disheartening when we do it in the eyes of the world. Because that's not how we are supposed to act as children of God. When we are the ones that are supposed to win souls for the kingdom of God. When we let our action form in a way that Jesus had walked in, the Holy Spirit will be within the day that has been written, and our spirit won't be in the wrong.

The day within the day is in Jesus. So all the moments that are within our day are not just the "same O thing, just a different day." It's a different day without the old things.

—John 16:33 (NIV)

The Day of the Meet

The day waiting to be met. When we meet up, what will we see, what will we talk about, and where will we meet? Only God knows the encounters we are going to have before leaving earth. So when it happens let's be on our best behavior for our Host of Host. It has to put a smile on God's face and joy in His heart. When we interact in life-filled conversations and enjoy righteous activities that warm the Holy Spirit. Also, the atmosphere gives Jesus a high five when our act of kindness is greater than His. The day of the meeting we are going to have in the days to come. They will be enriched! I (Cedric Easton) am looking forward to meeting you one day!

A day to meet is a day to speak what's on
your mind, heart, and soul.

—Romans 16:16 (NIV)

The Name of Today

When the day gives a name to him and her who have started to believe. At that moment he and she have a chance to live a life of sights of glorious wonder while counting all things with joy. Their hearts and minds will be in awe of all the things that come with believing in allowing Jesus to enter their lives. But they have to be careful of the non-believers when they get in the mood for worldly action in our relationship with God. We as God's children have to be there for the new him and her with open hearts and a judge-free faith in God. As they grow into the awe moment, they can live in the faith of Jesus and help others in their own awe.

When today starts to believe in us. That's
when we start to believe in today.

—Proverbs 22:19 (NIV); P.S.: Proverbs 22:17–21

The Day of Drink

Take a drink. In what way? In the rooms of my awesome and active family, we say, "One day at a time" and "the first one will take you out." To truly live life one day at a time, it takes a whole lot of courage to stand up. To the spirits that are contained in bottles and wrapped up in chaos. It's not easy to live with a no-nonsense-like mentality on the other side of life. There has to be a high tolerance for life that won't shame our friends, families, and loved ones. There are two liquid lies. The first is a life of chaos, shame, and regret. The second is the life of live water!

> The first drink will take you out of those
> places that are right next to the well.
>
> —Revelation 21:6 (NIV)

The Day Feels Like

We've all had that feeling where something is coming up, and we don't know how to approach it. I (Cedric Easton) had asked my pastor of Christian Fellowship Outreach Center at the time. He told me to ask God. What is this feeling? So I did that, and God made it clear, and I didn't let my emotions get in the way the next time that I felt that way. Now I have taken it steps further by asking God to prepare my mind, heart, and spirit right along with the wisdom and understanding.

Today will never feel like yesterday. Yesterday and today
will feel like tomorrow. Each has its own feeling.

—Matthew 26:21 (NIV)

The Actions

The day when actions are not our own. We all have had that moment in our day. When the actions of others get all out of sorts and our strong parts come unglued. As God's children, our actions are not to be wild and out like kids of this world. But sometimes we allow ourselves to act out the emotions, and it comes to the surface, and tends to lose our minds. But that does not mean we are not fit to be God's children.

It also doesn't give us the right to sweep it under the rug. Also, to let whatever happens is to fly out of control, which shows others how we really act in our faith when a problem erupts from the ashes. When we monitor our actions on a daily basis, traps will be set for us to fall at any given moment. But when our actions are altered by the works of our Father who is in heaven our life of light that Jesus had sprung in the world by His action will keep us out of the actions that are in sin.

A counselor told me something that will blow my mind for the
rest of my life. He said, "If I'm a hundred percent right, and
I act out inappropriately, I'm a hundred percent wrong."

—1 John 3:12 (NIV)

A Day in Between

A day that's in between our wants and needs. Some say that paying bills is a necessity of life that had to be done regardless of what's going on outside the home. That is a given rule if we want to live a life that is nice enough. But sometimes we just can't get right and hit that home run with our needs of life. And yet, as God's children He helps in our moment of need. So, we can enjoy our can't-get-rights even though we may have to sprint from base to base. Hoping our follies don't keep us from coming home. Our in-between is right there in the gap of other prayers.

There is a silver lining between us and in this world.

—Philippians 4:19 (NIV)

As the Day Speaks

We all know the saying, "If the walls could talk. What would they say?" The same goes here. What would the day say? From our actions, or when we are speaking to one another. The way we walk up to the person, how does the tone of our voice carry to another that puts them in a mood of reacting in a way that is righteous or an unsightly manner? Words are one of the most powerful things on this earth. Once we let it fly out, there are no words to force the retraction of negative statements. We can think of the kindest remarks to say to the one or ones who we've violated verbally. Even if we were on the other side of a rapid fire or a slow-burning lashing of hurtful words. Either way in that moment life is being turned upside down and a big stinger in the heart. What we say, how we say it, and the action behind it, it will have an everlasting moment in another's heart.

Words are the foundation on which life is supported.

—John 6:63 (NIV)

When the Day Has
Its Moments

When the day gets quiet on us! Some of us get nervous and forget to call on God and ask what is happening. Some of us don't even see the signs that are shown throughout the day or God within others trying to help. His voice is something that we know and come to count on when the trials and tribulations get too heavy. But what if it's one of those days that nothing has been shown to help us. What do we make of it? Some would think that God is far from them because they did something wrong. Others would say that there is a point in time where silence is golden. But when we talk to Him, there are numerous ways that we can go in silent places. Where there is spirit, no matter what we say or do, we have to remember that God will never leave us in a place of nothingness.

In the midst of our silence where the spirit of our day is. But the loudest of our peace is a blessing in the biggest bang of life.

—Psalm 107:28–30 (NKJV)

The Day Does Its Work

The day will work on its own all the way throughout us. But we will not know what the day is going to give us. Until God has given the day the proper work. Majority of the time it's beyond what we can do by planning on our own. The time God puts out on each day in us is all counted for. The things that come out of our actions and our motivation are not of us but of the Holy Spirit. The work we do in this world is not to be put on the back burner, and we cannot push God's work aside to live our life first. The word says, "Faith without work is dead." So whatever we do let's take that time to work on the things that God has given us to work on, while He works for us.

Putting our work before God shortens our life and all
that we do will be in long-suffering. It also will prolong
the agony, and all our actions of our own works.

—Ephesians 2:10 (NKJV)

Sunrise, Sunset with Tears

A farewell of a day. We all know that a farewell is the hardest to go through no matter the circumstances. It has been said that "time heals all." And yet the stronger the love is, the stronger the grief will be. With bonds like these, they are the hardest for the heart to let go of. Just think how the twelve disciples felt when Jesus died—they were devastated. Not only that He arose and was seen by their own eyes. Jesus spent time with them and then left again. It must have been disheartening to go through that. Now compare that to the farewells we deal with our family, friends, and those closest to our hearts. To me, I (Cedric Easton) wonder how long did it take them to *truly* get over Jesus's final farewell? To let go and let God is an understatement when letting go is the hardest thing to do in life and yet one of the *trust* actions we have to make so Jesus can heal us all.

A heartfelt goodbye from those who had lived a
life in the eyes of God warms the spirit. It comforts
the soul, and it puts the flesh at ease.

—Isaiah 41:6 (NKJV)

The Day Will Always See Us Through! Good Morning!

Goood morning, God's children! That's how I (Cedric Easton) imagine the day waking us up like that greeting us each by name. As we are stretching and yawning, do the usual things and then go about our business. Whether we're going to work, enjoying the day off by ourselves, or hanging out with loved ones. The biggest thing we do is our diligence while at work or just having a good time with others. Having a nice and peaceful solitude of a day.

Sometimes we forget to thank God for what He is doing at this moment. But of course we do remember that while with coworkers or surrounded by people we do take a long time and talk with God. We knew what to do and how to begin today and yet if we don't start off with Him. We will be bumping into each other with our eyes wide open. Missing out on blessings and not being able to hear His voice. We only know one thing about today—it is to rejoice and be glad about it.

To some of my brothers and sisters stop saying that I'm not
a morning person or I need a cup of coffee to be mobile
in the morning. God is our spring of life that wakes us
up with the joy-to-be-glad-in-it type of morning.

—Genesis 1:5 (NIV)

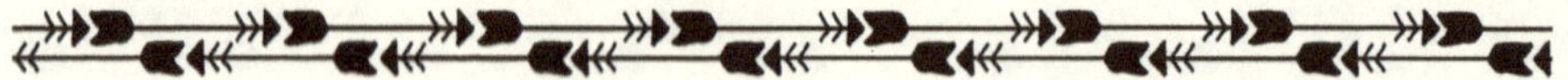

A Day of Living

In the rooms of being active and awesome. People find the strength, the power, and the courage to stay clear-headed—whatever it took to have a hopeful future. To live a life free from regret, selfishness, and a past full of shame. Taking the steps to get it right and stopping the madness to ask for help the mind wants a drop. It's not easy for a lot of people to step outside of the norm to be that motivated and search for opened doors or to grab their hands for assistance. For the truth to be told in all honesty an addiction out of sin and just living life go hand in hand. One, two, three, or even six steps are not enough. Now taking twelve steps or more will be needed. I'm not taking anything away from the people who are on the road to recovering or celebrating years by jumbling everyone together. Yet our greatest strength is coming to life. The best thing about this is the power of willingness.

Our higher power cannot be defeated. So He gives us the power
to defeat what the world can't overcome by themselves.

—Proverbs 27:17 (NIV)

The Day of Either or Either

The day that got away. When we get up from a good night's rest or a rough time of slumber, no matter what comes about our morning, it's either we get into God's word or not. Either way we go about our day nonchalantly or righteously. Wherever the wind blows is wherever we go, not stopping for the morning or cooling down in the day of the afternoon. But in the heat of today it matters how we are doing. The day is running without our hands of time, and yet sometimes we think of and look at today as we move about on what we are accomplishing or failing miserably at. But when we have a day that is filled with time that moves with quickness or the day that is in slo-mo, when we get such days like these, we are molded just as we are for that moment. On the day that is good, bad, or downright ugly let's not forget that today was not our day to keep in hand but to take heart and know that God got this day in His timing.

Good or bad, either or either, neither here nor
there, and in between or all over. The timing of the
day is in the hands of our Father of time.

—Zephaniah 1:12 (NIV)

P.S.: Why have they spelled the same way and yet said differently?

In Need

The day that wants to be in need. When we wake up there's an internal need to plan out the things that have to be done. So the rest of the day can move smoothly as possible. But most of us wait 'till the last moment to get it done. As adults we utilize our time in many ways shuffling from one thing to another. As believers we cannot allow the running of the day outweighing the needs that God wants us to do. Jesus's internal and external was all about focusing on the mission at hand. We have the same ambitions as Jesus had when He was walking in physical form. The need to change the outlook about how we utilize the timing that God has given us. I (Cedric Easton) am talking not only about myself (I, Cedric Easton, am a big procrastinator), but also about my brothers and sisters. Let's not let our timing be overrun by the big grand design after this world.

Our wants and needs are not small because God gave them to us.

—Psalm 20:4 (NIV)

A Hurtful and Rejoicing
of the Day

The day that hurts. At any moment pain can overwhelm the heart and consume it with unbearable hurt, and we don't know how to handle it. Hurt has a way of sewing emotions on the sleeves of those who are kind-hearted and don't like confrontation. Some even act out their hurt on others and in ways that have become their daily routine. It's the deepest wounds that will most likely never heal. Hurts are the greatest pain in life especially when our heart is hanging out in someone else's hands. Even as believers we only can handle what God gives us. But we cannot forget that Jesus has the biggest heart that ever walked on this earth. How deep are His wounds to His heart? And yet that would have not stopped Him from still loving us. So let's take the hurt from deep within our hearts and finally give it deep within God's capable and loving hands. So we can *rejoice* in days of hurt!

It's all kinds of hearts that go out of their way to be kind to another's heart. But it's a different kind of heart that acted out of true kindness when its own heart that's hurting.

—Psalm 9:2 (NIV)

Step Into

Today! Yeah, it knows itself! Today there are plans that are being met head-on, with hands and feet on the ground ready to hand in the paperwork we call life. When it's all said and done. We don't know what kind of grade we will be given or what kind of problems the next project will hold for us. Even though we've asked God for help we know that it comes in His timing. Sometimes we get a step ahead or just that quick our thinking goes outside the box instead of staying within the perimeters that God has provided.

There will be many outcomes that come with today. In the morning, will it arise with smiles or anger when the body goes to sleep? In our hearts and minds, will the storm settle throughout the day or well off into the night? We will have that time of peace and that moment to reflect on what God has given us. In the midst of the day that didn't have to transpire and mix with the night. We *cannot* allow ourselves to have a good morning and at the end of the night be shrouded in darkness or vice versa. God is the most gorgeous sunrise our eyes will see. The Holy Spirit keeps the fiery darts at bay and Jesus is the midnight Son.

When the day stops showing up, that's the day
when God says to Jesus, "It's okay time."

—Psalm 95:7 (NIV)

Go'n

When the day just goes, most mornings start right out of the gates and some the morning has a hard time starting their engines. While some just allow the breath of the morning to get them started. But there are the ones who speed through the morning like Superman and the Flash having a foot race. For the most part we allow so much to happen before a complete breakdown and not the loss of the mind. It's just from the exhaustion today has put on the body. We flip-flop from one thing to another. Whether we are on one task at a time or not. We are ever-changing throughout the day. We are not the same when we get to our households. Even the sluggard notices a difference. Sometimes we allow the goings-on to interfere with our standards in God and to let mental exhaustion take over us. That is a *big* no-no! The day goes wherever it goes, and we have to allow it because it belongs to God.

> Time is always flowing. It never sees the ending.
> Even in the midst of the day when we are standing
> still in the hands of the creator of time.

—Proverbs 21:31 (NIV)

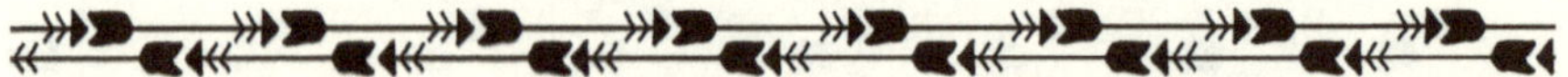

It's a New Day

That moment, in an instant, it happens. Where does it transpire? At the beginning of the morning, midday, evening, or somewhere throughout the night. God has done something and the newness under the sun. It shines brighter than a full moon; it twinkles more than all of the stars put together, deeper and richer than any colors that the rainbow can produce.

What God has done will be more dazzling than the lights in the darkened skies in the wonders of the universe. There is nothing new to God, and yet it's new to us; that's a no-brainer. But what happens to the saying? "There's nothing new under the sun." But I (Cedric Easton) think that only applies to God, not to us. God is the same today, yesterday, tomorrow, and forevermore. All things are new to us; it even says it in His word. "Sing a new song, new wine, a new creation, and a new thing," says the Lord. So, that newness comes from heaven and that new breath that He breathed in. (2 Corinthians 2:4; Ezekiel 36:26).

Same old, same old. Just a different day. Has no
wonder work in a child of God's life?

—Ecclesiastes 1:9 (NIV)

The Day that Is over There and Here as Well

When it's that kind of day. Most will never know about the world of meetings. The active and awesome people that go through the day are strapped to a roller coaster that does not stop. We cannot allow the twelve footprints to get lost in the steps of this world. In the moment that we are unaware while in the grits and grinds of the day. When our minds start to unravel, things seem to be way outside of the rules and thrown out the window. Our feeling has that type of mindset. It's not just about the substance of sin. It's whatever has a hand on our lives that replaces the hands of God. Truly.

On days that take us up to the top and with no warnings…drop us with a force that brings tears to our eyes, as the wind smashes into our faces. But it's not just addiction, in which we are taken by surprise. It is this sudden change of loop-the-loops, the upside-downs, and sometimes reverse of a ride. We all will get the chance to experience these phenomena of afflictions that plagues us in moments that come in various and unfortunate ways. Our struggles are different, but the meetings are the same. So when we or others say, "I got this in the bag," be aware because when that kind of a day shows up we should not forget what we are going to do, and what God is doing.

There is nothing to forget about this day. So, let's not focus on the losses, and let's grab hold of the victories.

—1 John 4:4 (KJV)

Holy Spirit! I Think I Need Your Help on This One

The day of many. Which one is chosen? Everyone has an opinion, and the majority of them are useless. But what if it worked out? Then doesn't it mean that the opinion becomes a factual statement? For me (Cedric Easton) it makes it factual, but it is just my opinion. As for the ones who worked out those opinions that turned them into action, they kept them from sailing into false and empty moments. They put them into a run-down and shipwrecked situation of life. Now here comes wisdom, and understanding weeds them out, while discernment helps transform it into likely or unlikely. I (Cedric Easton) like it when a pastor says, "Don't take my word on what I just said, but look at it for yourself."

> An opinion has been put to the test throughout the
> world today. But God is the only one that knows
> the percentage of failing and the passing rate.
>
> —1 Corinthians 7:6 (NIV)

A Day without a Camera Crew, True Reality

When the day captures the eyes, what a sight to be seen. A sight to be held in the retinas. It moderates our faith in God, and even more so it strengthens our characters in our Christ-like family. But for some, believing is impossible without seeing it firsthand and especially when they are in the midst of it all.

When this marvelous thing takes place something happens to us. Sometimes it can be overwhelming from where we are sitting to when we are standing because we couldn't contain ourselves. As the eyes go transform the doll to amazement moving from side to side. We can see God shifting in this place of awareness that reaches deep within us.

For example, I (Cedric Easton) was sitting in a place called the Rope Center that helps with addiction, homeless, and rehousing, among other things. I was sitting straight back in the left corner eating, and my eyes were seeing something I couldn't explain. Everybody was getting their needs met with clothes, shoes, socks, food—the list goes on and on. But this was bound just giving out the necessities. The place was just filled with joy. It was like everyone had it all together. People rarely get to see the lost; they have pure joy while being homeless. The volunteers there have so much heart that they did everything to help us in every way they possibly could to get us through this moment in our lives. Christ is at its finest.

Waking up in the midst of the storm will change the
atmosphere when we stand up like Jesus did in the
boat and spoke peace that comes from within.

—Matthew 25:36–40 (NIV)

Past Days

Our past always has many ways of popping up and stopping us in our tracks or keeping us from having victory over it. For some it's hard to let go of the past when hate and anger are all they have. For most it gives them the power even if knowing that's an illusion they still hold on to it. It's sad, and yet the funny part of it all is when the world tells us that believing in something you see is silly. But what they don't know is that God gives us the strength to handle our back in the day transgressions.

Our past is a touchy subject so much hurt, pain, and sorrow that most *cannot* get rid of it. Food for thought: David, Peter, and Paul. David is a murderer among other things but still entangled with God's heart. Peter denied Jesus, and yet His shadow was healing people as He walked by. Paul will we know that he was stricken blind for killing co-heirs to the throne and was blessed by beginning on fire for God. I (Cedric Easton) want to say thank you God for my touchy subject and for not allowing my past to beat me down than it already had. So with that being said we can stand tall at the end of our past or fall at the beginning of the future.

Oh yeah! Fun fact: Moses is a very close
friend of God, and he's a murderer.

—Job 17:11 (NIV)

At This Moment Today Is

This is now a life thought. What worries us throughout the day? What is the biggest thorn in our side? Let's get the cat out of the bag. Questions like these in the midst of a trying week are understandable. And yet, blessing will *not* fall on us while we are in the house of self-turmoil. Worrying is a *big* no-no! There's nothing worse than a child of God being a prisoner of doubt. God is not going to hold our hands and walk us to the sandbox of despair, nor will He push us on the swings, so we can jump off the edge, and last but not least He will not allow us to sleep at His feet while angry at our brothers and sisters.

I (Cedric Easton) now understand the feeling of what God has put in me. Now when it is up and arises in me, I ask God to let me know what this feeling is and what it means. I also ask Him to give me the wisdom and understanding on how to get through these weary days.

Worrying takes the power away from God. That's one thing that God is not going to be while in heaven nor on this earth.

—Matthew 11:28–30 (NIV)

Day of Time

Hours are gone, and the days keep adding up. If we could count how much time we've put into the things that were not of God, we'd lose all sense of time. To get back what can never be returned. We know now that time is not our own, and that time is its own. God wakes us up each and every morning without excuses. So we can have a chance to get it right one more. We have to allow God to work in our lives in His timing. We all know that time is everything to us, and yet we also know that God is not bothered by it.

I (Cedric Easton) used to think of all the time I've wasted on myself, among other things, and the most was not giving it to God. It used to mess with me a lot, but one of the pastors who I came across in my life taught me a lesson. She said, "Don't think of the time you've lost that you didn't give to God, but think of what you are doing now." It helped me out immensely in ways that build me up. To do things and to keep on moving forward. To do God's will, to live in His way, to speak His word, and to do His works.

Time in God is time living out of this world, and
time of this world is not the time we need.

—1 Chronicles 12:22 (KJV)

One, Two, Three Days

Seconds, minutes, and hours in a day. It's counted up into a week, and yet nothing really matters in what we did in those moments, except for the actions we've done to sharpen one another. We've spent time and effort on a lot of things in our lives. Some of these things may have put a smile on God's face. There are few people we run into that truly have a heart with a kind of love that we can see in their eyes, with a handshake and a hug to match. To see the kind of love in the actions without looking for an outward wealth in others' eyes but in God's. Living a kind of life like that after living a life of selfishness. The seconds, minutes, and hours will be destroyed in a matter of moments. With the time of selflessness love for one another will be greatly respected in the eyes of heaven.

As we love in the midst of God, the time in
heaven will be well-spent on earth.

—Matthew 22:37–39 (NIV)

In the Heart of the Day

In the heat of the moment, a word from a righteous heart can restore and lift a life that was deep in death. It also can kill all the things that are not of God at the same time. The words of life keep us in check in all the paths that lead us righteously. When it seems like the light of life is getting dim, when we are at our weakest and don't know where to go, the words of the righteous will shine through the pages, strength will be given, and the footprints will be multiplied as they guide us through the valleys.

The day does not start until the heart has spoken.

—John 6:63 (NIV)

Move It! Move It! Move It!

Moving along as fast or slow as it can. As one day turns into two, three moved on to four, and as the weekend starts. Monday's sun began to rise upon us. Just before we all knew it, seven days had passed, and the weekend seems like it never got a chance to slow down so we couldn't take a breather. Meanwhile, some weeks are so slow that we can count the seconds on the weekend as the air flows through our lungs. All the stress, pain, sorrow, joys of laughter, and spending time with our loved ones. The emotions will run high in any situation and can drastically turn from good to bad in a matter of seconds, and the worse may get a chance to show up. No matter what comes our way, we know that the hands of God keep us moving forward and the days to come.

We can't get caught up in woe. I am a child of God. When things get intertwined and go sideways, murmuring and complaining take moments away from the times of joy within the soul.

—Proverbs 24:10 (NIV)

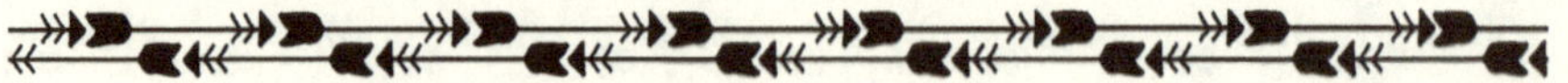

Love This Moment, in These Days

Here is the moment that God has given. When we have the chance to pray for others in a mass sitting or one on one. The time to watch and to look into the days of wisdom and understanding is in our hands. It is a privilege and honor to be in this position. Our Father allows us to go out in His will, to speak His words, to do it in His way, and to do His works. To help our sisters and brothers live in a new level of faith and at the same time encourage ourselves. To have a breakout moment in His love for others as well as the participants. We leave new trails in our lives just as Jesus did when He was in the flesh. The Father, Son, and the Holy Spirit live in us. We just have to activate the power that has been stored up in us onto others!

By God, for us, to give to others. What is it _________________?

—Deuteronomy 30:16 (NIV)

In the Times of Each Day

    In our timeline that's not on Facebook, but in the step that we've taken, in the time we've lived, and what we have done with it, can we truly say that the times we did spend on the important things of God for us? To give to others that truly were in need with the discernment to let God handle what we could not. As the times awaken in our memories of what we've done and in the manner it was done in, can we say "job well done" without being self-centered in God's eyes? I (Cedric Easton) do know one thing that we have to keep doing—putting a smile on God's face.

In the meantime, let's make sure that in the end,
we have filled Jesus with joy. He died for us.

—Colossians 3:23 (NIV)

The Truth about Today

In today's love and letting go. My sisters and brothers, when a loved one is out of control and words from the heart are fanning the flames, there's nowhere to go, and no one to turn to except for a program. That may or may not be the umpteenth time. We all know there is a place in time where letting go in the hands of God is best.

But letting go of a person who is the best thing to the one that's holding on to is the truest form of love that can be given on that day. I (Cedric Easton) firsthand know what it's like to be let go in love because of my drugging and drinking. We don't have the right to dismiss anybody out of our lives without the permission of God's love. When the addiction gets stronger, God's love will develop deeper in the hearts of His children. And for our family members that are still out there trapped in the whirlwind of alcoholism and habitual drug abusers. God wants to throw a homecoming party in the honor of His children.

When we pour alcohol into ourselves selfishly we pour our true selves into the bottle wholeheartedly. When drugs are taken the mind gets weakened and soberly thoughts are hidden. Both of them combined spiritually poison the roots within the body.

—Galatians 6:1 (NIV)

In the Middle of the Day as Life Become

The past days became weeks. We all know that when time passes it gets closer and closer. Soon it will be at the end of the month. We've all had that self-expression of asking ourselves. Where did the time go? As soon as we say these words the end of the year is here. I (Cedric Easton) know that a lot of God's children don't like telling their ages, but every second that passes a day has gone, another week is approaching, and the year is rapidly coming closer and closer. But majority of us know that we've done very little for the kingdom of God. and we don't want to leave this earth without doing something impactful. In the minutes that are drawn near in the weeks, months, and years to come, I (Cedric Easton) have put it into my heart that before I leave this earth I want to put a smile on God's face as Noah did. When we end the week and start anew it's all about what we've given unto God throughout that past week into the weekend.

Our start is our own, just like our ending but our zeal is
the same. To be Christ-like all through the middle.

—James 2:14–26; James 2:14 (NIV); Proverbs 16:31 (NIV)

P.S.: So don't lie or hide the wonderful splendor that life has given.

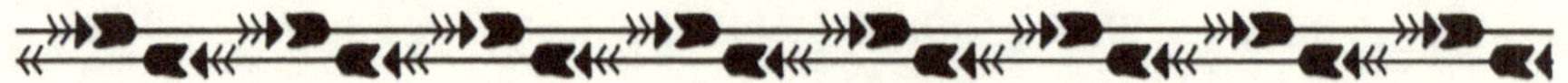

The Step In and Step Out of Days

As we take the steps from day to day and into the weekend, the passing moments will be washed away by fresh footprints on the beach. We have to take the time to relax our mind and give our bodies the rest it needs. Because our to-do list is longer than what we can handle. Even when one task is being taken care of, some still can get overwhelmed with it. We all know another one will start sooner or later and we could lose focus.

If we allow ourselves to move through the day by ourselves without asking for help, we can take a step back when we do things on our own as children of God. Taking steps backward is not an option when going forward and yet when we stab our toe in sin. It's not to reflect on what was done but on what to do about it now. Stabbing our toe is a negative step backward to most but that's only without repentance. We look back on moments in life or days that just passed. It's to glance at what God has done for us within the midst of life's monkey wrenches and curve balls.

When we fall steps are taken to get back up. It could take days, weeks, months, and up to years to see the wonderful works our faith in God has plans that have for us.

—Psalm 37:23 (NIV)

P.S.: Stepping back in the past without a productive outlook will take the body back right it left off. But stepping out of the past is to have faith in what's to come.

Today's Mishaps

The day worked itself out. We know that this is the day that the Lord has made. When the day starts, we start our regular routine and then we head out into the world as God's children. With no shortcuts just a whole lot of favor. No matter where we go as long as our steps are ordered by God we will be more than okay.

Case in point: one day I (Cedric Easton) was riding the bus to fill out a job application and left my bookbag on the bus. I thought it was going to be a bad day, but the thought quickly left my head because I know that God had me. I got my cell phone and called the bus operator to tell the driver what happened. I rode my bike as fast as I could to the stop station.

As I was getting close the bus had pulled off onto the road and up to the red light. I was still on the phone with the operator and she is communicating with the driver so I pulled up to the bus. The driver opened up the door, and my bookbag was given to me with all my belongings.

Two things happened. One of the people on the bus knew who I was, and they automatically told the diver about my bookbag. I also have to believe that it was the kind of person God had made into being kind and loving toward others. The second thing that went down was the job I went to. I was asked to speak to the manager, and she came up to me. We exchanged pleasant greetings and talked about the jobs they had for hire. The conversation was outstanding! All in all I just had forgotten what had just happened before I came in. I just know that when we put it in God's hands our mishaps fall into the gap of the forgotten.

At the beginning and all the way to the end we know somewhere
in the middle that the tools will be working in our favor as
long as we work the step on leveling up to our faith.

—Jude 20 (NIV)

Days of Forgetfulness

Sometimes I (Cedric Easton) forget the things that have been done to me and things I've done to others, not because I don't want to but because I grew up the way I did living in foster care. Basically I was a ward of the state that has never been adopted. I was also drinking and doing drugs. I've had memory lapse. My mind had kept me from remembering things that might have the potential to do me some harm. Sometimes I want to remember but then again maybe it's a good reason that I don't. We all know that God has that kind of mind to throw our sins away. We have a scapegoat to pour our days that we want to forget as children of God, especially the ones that went through traumatic experiences. We do have the luxury to smile in our memories because of our remembrance of what Jesus did in His past to ensure our future.

No matter what, when we cannot remember something. Jesus is always there shining His light on a darken thoughts.

—Colossians 3:1–17(3:2) (NIV)

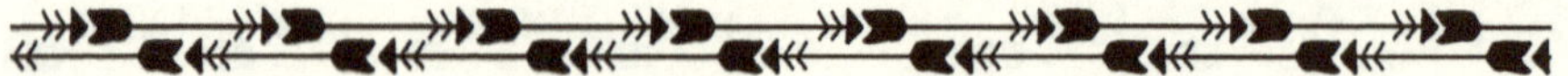

Blah of a Day

What a day. There is a saying that most people say when they are having a blah of a day. They utter the words, "It is what it is or I can't call it." When these days occur it's not having a good or bad day. It's just the in-between. We've all had a day like this but to describe the day as a mundane thing is not to be taken lightly.

God's children should never speak of today as if it's a round-about day that has no meaning. When this moment arrives, what should we say? How should we react when people ask us how our day is going? There is so much that happens in these moments. We just cannot allow anything to come out of our mouths to the world. On days like these, we run the risk of people thinking that God's children are ungrateful and do not enjoy the in-betweens of a rundown day.

It is safe to say that Jesus didn't have an off day, but He
did have off moments. When people, places, and things of
the day tried to get Him offset and out of character.

—James 1:3 (KJV)

Within the Day

To love and to cherish this day, we all know that fear is a force to be reckoned with. It kills all things in life. Fear warps the mind, poisons the soul, and tears the spirit apart. Nothing grows in the midst of fear. It just gets stronger and stronger each and every day with hatred that is shared equally with the darkness. When we enter that place, the still small voice turns into a noise of emptiness, of carelessness, with mindless love for chaos and destruction. To defeat it from the bottom to the top, the love of God is all that we need to inject into our lives. His love is like a black hole. It sucks all that is His in, and what comes out on the other end is His light of life.

To cherish the love like today is to jump into
the heart of God and fade away.

—Isaiah 41:10 (NIV); Psalm 36:7 (NIV)

P.S.: Scientists' theory on the other side of a black hole is a light hole.

Be Glad and Enjoy!

Oh, happiness into today! When we wake up and move about our day we know that at the start of a good or great and awesome day, is to get it in, in any kind of way that pleases, and to show approval to God. We are not to take it upon ourselves to fix anything because the day is already put together, in ways we can't even imagine. We also know that in the midst of it all, a gloomy storm is coming no matter what we do. So we ask God in so many ways to help us through these moments. A good, bad, or just downright ugly day is always around the corner, but so is God. So no matter what we do at the beginning of our day, it all hinges on. If we allow God to express the joy and love He has made into today.

When hardship is pressed on a person, it's difficult to jump, hop, and skip with a smile on the face. It's even disheartening witnessing others have joy while in a tough situation, when anxiety and stress overwhelm the mind of the person that cannot cope with what's going on. Now many of God's children won't let it get that far but either way, life has its drawbacks. So let's not draw ourselves back into the way of the world where words like joy are for the wealthy.

—2 Corinthians 4:16 (NIV)

A Little, a Lot. No,
Just Enough

The day that holds just enough. We all know that God does not give us more than what we can handle, and His time of help will come, the time that we spend at home, school, work, or just hang out with friends, family, and loved ones. We have no idea what's around the corner. We all are hopeful that good times just keep on rolling, but that's just wishful thinking. Even though more often than not, mishaps do occur in our lives. God has given us the tools to handle humanely situations without divine power. But without warning here it comes. Boom! Chaos starts to rampage! The home is in disarray, and pencils and paper are flying all over the place. The boss has their foot on the gas and won't let up. Friends, family, and loved ones aren't there for moral support. To most people all seems lost. Sometimes a child of God does lose sight but unlike others that had a play-play relationship with God. Know that hardship can come out of nowhere.

Being a child of God is not an easy life, and
yet it's a wonderful life. Enjoy!

—Ephesians 6:10 (NIV)

The Day of Chaos to Peace

The day that transformed from chaos to peace, when the man slung the young lady to the underground in front of Jesus. We all know the story but for my brothers and sisters that do not (John 8:1–11 NIV). Jesus said to them, "Let any one of you who is without sin be the first to throw a stone at her." After speaking He stooped down and began to finish His writing in the sand. Really no one knows what He was writing.

I (Cedric Easton) like to think that question will be answered while in heaven. But what I want us to focus on is Jesus's demeanor about the whole situation from start to finish. He never lost His composure. He didn't yell or scream in frustration at the accusers. Even when He spoke to the young lady His emotions stayed the same. In the face of someone's death, Jesus remained calm. It's easy reading it and then acting it out. That kind of calmness Jesus displayed.

Our ability to be that calm is greater than we give ourselves credit.

—Ecclesiastes 10:4 (NIV)

Today I Will Flight or Fight

The flight or fight is an act that will grip us all. The heart is beating fast, palms are sweating, feet are like concrete and yet can be lifted like a house easily moved by the wind! The mind tries to collect a thought, but they are all over the place! The body is in a massive overload of multiple anxiety attacks! Not too many of us have been to that extreme of being stressed out, but we have inhaled a small whiff of that kind of disarray. As God's children we rarely lose our GPS in a fight-or-flight situation, but when we do our compass of faith points toward God. God won't allow the chemicals of our bodies to go into fight-or-flight mood without the right balance. His power will help us have victory. To flee from the situation or be the firm foundation!

Fighting without a cause is weak and fleeing with a purpose is not.

—Ephesians 6:4 (NIV)

Days of Days in Prayer

The day when our words are recognized in the eyes of heaven. As we sit, kneel, or lay down—whichever is comfortable to us— prayer is about to be committed. As we finish the prayer, our words are on a journey far, far, far away beyond the stars further than any Milky Way. As it lands in the earlobes of our Father they get deciphered from right now into later on. And one day just like that, all of our words will come face to face with reality. I (Cedric Easton) have heard that we shouldn't pray for ourselves but for others because God already knows what we need, but we know better then. It's a magnificent moment when the day finally happens of being persistent in prayer and the windows of heaven are pouring a blessing out on us.

By standing firm and faithful, the room of receiving will
be expanded so far beyond the point of no return. That
the overflow will be in the generations to come.

—Ephesians 6:18–20 (NIV)

The Day of Truth

The truth is spoken without words. They say actions speak louder than words, and it has been proven throughout the lives that share that concept. I (Cedric Easton) was in a program that helped me realize who I am in God's eyes. While I was in class, the instructor quoted the famous line, "Everyone likes to use about actions and words." He took it a step further by saying, "We read the words and then put them into action. But whose words are we using? The world's or God's words?" The world has a truth about its standards and holds on tightly to what it says. So the actions of this world, no matter how right it is, do not hold up to the righteousness that is in us.

Our actions are bold no matter, whether they're being loud
in a concert or subtle like a mouse sneezing in a cotton
ball. The truth will be active throughout the day.

—1 John 3:18

For Today the Morning Stars!

A morning that is in the latter days of sunshine. A clear blue sky or everlasting clouds floating above us and as the sun hangs high in the sky. As fluffy whites linger from the sky, the heart says, "thank you" and gives God all the glory on days like these. Even though we know that somewhere evil wants to have its moment in our day of relaxing in God's glory, we also know that rejoicing in the bad days will lead up to even greater fluffy whites than the last. We will never see a more truthful morning than this.

As a child we've seen. As pre-teens we've taken a glance. As teens we've looked at it. As young adults we've had time to marvel at it and as fully grown cherish it. Because living that long we never know when the next sunset or sunrise will be the last.

—Ecclesiastes 7:14 (NKJV)

Today While Waiting!

That one day when the day of time ceases to exist. No matter where we are there will be a moment of time when waiting patiently is key. When waiting on something or someone time is not only the factor. Our emotions play a big part in the waiting game of life. Waiting is one thing that will bring out the good, the bad, and the downright ugly side of a person's mindset. A person can only be so good when it comes to waiting in line. Let the elderly go ahead, a mother with kids, a person digging in their purse or wallet for loose change.

Being at a red light eight cars behind, the turn signal is green, and no one is moving. The horn is blown out of a slight frustration. Now it's red. Just a few more seconds, and that person would have gotten through if the first car paid attention. Now that is the moment when the good turned into bad, and here it comes. There is no time now that an old person can wait, seeing the mother having a hard time with the kids and putting the groceries in the car. The person looks but doesn't want to help because of that red turn signal. What that person doesn't know is if the he spent time waiting in line and helping the mother, they may not have been in that ugly car accident. Now the elderly person and the mother with kids are praying that everyone's okay.

They say time waits for no man or woman. One of
the truest statements ever said on this earth. But when
patience is not of this earth the timing is nowhere
to be found in the hands of man or woman.

—Joshua 10:13 (NIV)

P.S.: They say patience is a virtue, but it's not. It's a job, so we have to work on it.

Today I Listened

Whether it is moseying alone, very slowly or struck like a match, when the day starts it comes with a force which nothing on this earth can stop. Today is already wrapped up. It's even tied up with a red bow and sent into the present. When the day comes it's very new in every way imaginable that's under sunrise and sunsets. But under all of this newness there is something that has to be brought up.

When we ask someone how they are doing today, we do have an obligation not to poke or prod into those lives but to be genuinely honest about asking someone's feelings about the day they're having. So much so, that they can hear the earnestness of the request in our voice. When our spirit, soul, and body get built up we need to release it. Whether the response is good, bad, or so-so kind of a day. But it's paramount that on this day that God has given us. That we need the Holy Spirit to lead in every second of this conversation so they will feel comfortable and release the thing that is on their heart.

Just listening with our ears is not enough.

—Proverbs 11:14 (KJV)

When They Have Changed

Every day is that moment. Palm Sunday. The moment when everything changed. When Jesus came in the way He was acknowledged by everyone. He did not boast or want to seek attention on what He had done already or is about to do. His action spoke volumes, and He allowed Himself to be seen without aggression on His part. But He displayed the authority to shake the foundations of faith in the law and the leaders of the church. He moved about freely, in a way He wanted to with respect and honor for the Father in heaven. Leading up to the day to where He said, "It is finished," He showed us how to act in the midst of hostile moments and to have love for others when they are assassinating our character. Jesus opened up the way for us to do more with the power that has been given to us.

In a world where it's being so loud. We can
still be heard while speaking so softly.

—Matthew 5:18 (NIV)

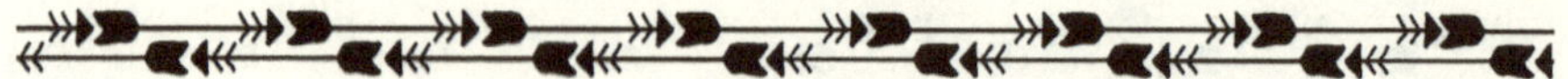

Today Is When We...

To have others understand that our faith in the works has been given to us is pivotal. To each and every moment that they spend time hearing and watching us, for us to be understood in what we say and do to the work that has been given to us. Also, in action, our faith portrays the work that has been done in us. We are not perfect... Interruption! Interruption!

In the mind the reader says, "Duh. Cedric, we all know that." Then the writer says, "Will you excuse me for pointing and writing out something so obvious when trying to be coy about a statement?" The writer also says, "I hope someone found that small snippet of writing amusing." But on the lighter side of trying to be funny, most people don't realize that we are made perfect out of God's love. We also try to do our best to allow the Holy Spirit to override our opinion by stating facts about the things in the Bible to them. So we don't have to be emotional and humanely driven to drive the point across.

Going outside to play is nothing when we enjoy the work we do.

—Proverbs 12:14 (NIV)

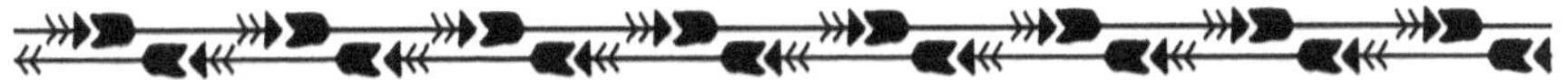

When Today Matches the Out with the In

Being happy is an outward action. That feeling best described when the flesh is down and out. But joy is an inside job, working within the soul because a Child of God allowed the spirit to be fed first. Most of the time people don't know when they are in the presence of unique individuals who are active and awesome whom I am glad to be a family member.

Before we became a member, our flesh was full of doom and gloom. We also allowed foul taste to bring us joy to fulfill the emptiness that is within our souls. And in the least that we've made, last is our spirit being clouded and swimming in the midst of other spirits. But when that opportunity came our way, we seized the moment and arose to the occasion. We grabbed the little hope of chance to have faith in being sober-minded. Entering the family for the first time was an eye-opener. But God allowed us to understand that we will find our inter joy in this awesome and active family that He created for His children. No matter what family we belong to, the bloodlines lead to the body of Christ.

Without a reason to be bubbling over with life, but we will always have a reason to have blackouts in death.

—James 1:2 (NIV)

Today Is the First Time

When a negative and a positive from a battery get hooked together, power is formed. Remember the first time of being so nervous in the act of being a Christian. When we felt in our hearts through helping others or stepping out into faith on life's biggest decisions. That time when we stood up to being bullied by an evil spirit with the power of God. The first time when it looked like there was no way out, and all of a sudden the light hits us in the face. *Boom*!

There are so many experiences of first-timers we've had that only God can count up. But this is one of my favorites. When we give without expecting anything in return, and God opens up the windows of heaven for an on-time blessing. Nowadays we are just that bold. By standing at the throne God is talking with others who have yet to make the decision to become a member of the family. He is helping the younger sisters and brothers get through their cloud-nine-euphoria moments and above all those who are working together to escape from their negative hookups, to the most positive power we can connect to.

To do nothing in His name is to do everything in this world.

—1 Timothy 5 (NIV)

Which Way Did the Day Go?

The waters rushing down the streams of life. The sun shines on one side and rains on the other. The stillness of the night, the love that twinkling in the midnight sky. The wind of encouragement crashed into hearts. With the sound of a newborn crying in the wilderness walking on a foundation that will not crumble. Tries of pain race from the soul, while tries of love are near the spirit. While the mind thinks of worries, instantly it becomes a fleeting thought. Sometimes we have days where it's like a whirlwind of strange and beautiful things.

Saying "That's crazy" is not how eyes see or judge
it to be crazy but how we receive it.

—Song of Solomon 4 (NIV)

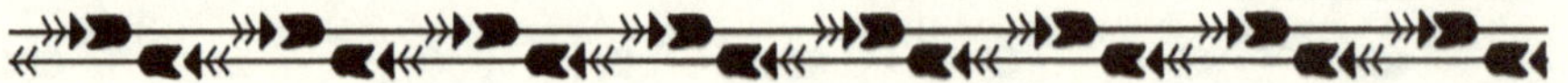

The Day When We Can

What's mine is mine. We know this to be true in every way shape and form no matter how it comes. But sometimes we don't get the desire of our hearts, and we ask, "Why?" Even when we are as righteous as we can be yet God hasn't yielded. We also know that it's all in His timing or it's not beneficial to us. It's deep-rooted in us as a child of God in knowing that He can and will. But sometimes we forget that it's not all about what God can do for us.

A pastor once said, "We are always asking Him for something. Sometimes we should be asking, 'What can I do for You in Your honor, God?'" It may sound crazy and outside of the box because we give Him all the glory, honor, and praises. What else can we do? I (Cedric Easton) had prayed a prayer with that in mind. What can I do for you, God? And He answered me days later. He told me to just keep on doing what I do in my name. I (Cedric Easton) know people out there say, "Be careful what you pray for. God will answer you accordingly to what you ask for." Well, I (Cedric Easton) am glad He said what He said.

Helping God in every way we can will
allow us to love each other more.

—1 Samuel 3:9 (NIV)

The Power in the Days to Come

Power to plan without thought hurdles. The power to speak from the heart without words. The power to be meek and humble. The power to do the things that the eyes cannot believe. The power to walk on water and through floods. The power to do your will, Father, and the power to deny my flesh. But above all else to have faith in your son, Jesus! To be bold and ask for this is not overdoing it. Sometimes we cut ourselves short and wonder why we can't see or do more.

We already fall short because of sin. Let's not
go beyond the trapdoor in our prayers.

—James 5:16 (NIV)

The Day

A renewed mind, being pure at heart and faith like a child. But first love no other gods and love thy neighbor, like you love yourself. Some know better than others how hard life is and how easy it is to quit on everything in life. To live without love for life and the things of it all. When it gets so hard for most, they think that God is not on their side. That He had forgotten them and so relied on the world to get them through, with them not knowing that God is there in those programs—they just have to open up and see Him. God is enough. He tells us in His words on how to live a righteous life and all the blessings that come with facing hardships. God has a plan for a hopeful future, and we are in the design.

The darkness is always going to be there. But it runs
into the next room when the light comes on.

—Psalm 107:13–14

What Do Know about Today

In the midst of the unknown is where great and wonderful things happen. What is so beautiful and dangerous about the unknown? It's like tomorrow we don't know what's coming. We can stay up all night and see the sunrise, yet tomorrow still has to come. Even though we figured it out and can do a hundred projects just like it, the outcome will still be the same, and the unknown factors will get greater than the last. But the greatest part is the fact that wisdom and understanding took place, by not giving in on tomorrow's problems or allowing the next project's trials and errors to get the mind all in a frenzy.

If not knowing keeps a person safe and knowing may destroy
a person, then the unknown will put them both in limbo.

—Matthew 24:36–39 (NIV)

We All Helped Out Today!

Helping someone who has nothing. Let's just say that God is sitting back waiting until the time is right. He reaches down and grabs our hand to help someone out. It's out of norm of life but not unrealistic. When it comes to helping our sister or brother suffering from an altered state of mind or drowning in the sorrows of the liquid viper. There is no way we can go haphazard with a request like this. God is definitely going to the max. He will turn this earth upside down like a woman, shaking her purse and trying to get her favorite lip gloss. For us to go that deep we wield the power of God, wisdom, and understanding to give that kind of hand helping maneuvering skills that He has. Sometimes it takes a lot, and sometimes it takes a whole heck of a lot. We are not in it for the long haul but we are for a short lifetime.

A packet of jumbled-up words that's full of life can
save a person's life. Then we do need smooth talkers
to give us cheat code to get out of the grave.

—Romans 8:28 (NIV)

Who's Driving Today?

Staring into the rearview mirror and not realizing that some people are calling for help. Others are trying to get occupant attention, but they did not prevail. But there was nothing they could really do. God only gives us so much that we can handle. When He tells us to back off from helping someone, that's one request that we cannot ignore, even if we think that person almost got it or just needs a little more time to start to focus on their life. And yet, God, you want me to stop? If we are truly, true in God in letting us make that decision to let a friend, a family member, a loved one, or someone that truly close to our heart go, then I thank God for the Holy Spirit because letting go like that can devastate a person to the point of no return. We all know that God has a reason for everything and by letting that person(s) go, it frees us from the heavy burden that Jesus is supposed to carry. I (Cedric Easton) have been on both sides of the spectrum.

God gives us the power to do anything in life but when
He still wants us to back off that power is gone.

—Matthew 27:46 (KJV)

P.S.: Letting go is a multitude of things. So let go of that one lying in the hospital bed and let them go home to the Father. Oh, doesn't God promise if He keeps that person here on earth it may not end up the way it is given?

Today We Will

The fast-paced day. To meet the day with full steam ahead out into the wilderness we. To see everyone moving from place to place with or without God. It's amazing to know when to stand still and go about the day that is given. We know that the world does not take time out to smell the roses. We also know that a lot of our brothers and sisters are very impatient even though they know that's one of the fruits of the spirit. We definitely know that time doesn't wait for no man or woman, but we try to do our best to get the things on the do list, with time allotted.

As children of God we've been chosen to do what is necessary in order to show others that we are leaders. Wise men and women that know how to handle the things that the world throws at us. Let us *not* forget! That the word of God will show up in us. That we can be that light which Jesus displayed.

To slow down and gather the thoughts is a wonderful thing but
to allow them to impact the life of another is now heavenly.

—Acts 6:1–7 (NIV)

P.S.: Don't forget that we all have gifts from God to display to the world.

This Is What Today Said to Me

Living in the moment only to grip the experience to live a clean life. You can take yourself seriously. Just don't take the fun out of living because you're so serious. Be careful when changing for the better because greater tragedies are smiling with joy and its heart. Even though chaos can be calculated it is still chaos; there's no way around it. Being a family member of an awesome and active family, we have a lot of quotes to keep us focused when our mind begins to wander off into the land of *ooh*s and *aah*s.

A good way to end the day is by saying
something encouraging to myself.

—1 Thessalonians 5:11 (NIV)

Today Nature Has Spoken!

Like a blanket of snow with every flake as unique. Like a tree deep-rooted lavished with exquisite leaves that are not like the one beside it. Water so still that every living creature in it has serenity. Their counterparts on land join them in prayer as they trot by. As the winds whistle a new song through the wings that graces the sky. Every living creature has a gift, and they use it to their full potential for us to see.

As the sun rises and as the sunsets a star gets gazed upon by the moon and the moon smiles as the last bit of light from the day.

—Luke 19:40 (NIV)

What Going to Happen Today?

Knowing what the day brings and still being surprised by what's going to come from is one of the most wonderful and dazzling feelings but also terrifying. It's like throwing a surprise birthday party, and that person knows it but doesn't know where or who are going to be there. Also, knowing a person is going to leave this earth knowing who Jesus is and not accepting Him now is terrifying. It is mind-blowing to know that one moment can have two outcomes.

To choose one knowing that there's more is disheartening
to the ones that could not choose at all.

—2 Timothy 1:7 (KJV)

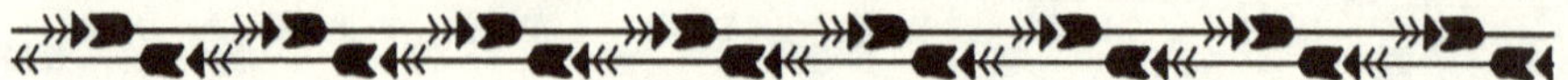

Today We Stand and Fight

To be in a fight without throwing a blow is almost non-existent. A one-on-one fight with both sides is preparing for battle. The armor is assembled and being put on. The rest is well needed, and yet one of the opponents is going to be sluggish. When we go to war as a child of God we don't have the luxury to sit back and let Jesus do all the work. We have to stand and allow the world to see that the word of God is powerful. When we put our faith to work the damage we will receive will be minimal. But it also depends on what we are having faith in. Some of God's children don't have to do much, and they're off to another battle or they are resting. Meanwhile, some are in the same battle for years because of doubt.

A bell starts the fight, and it also ends the rounds…

—2 Corinthians 10:4 (NIV)

A Gift for Today

A seed soon while being sober will have strong roots in life. The wisdom, understanding, and love from others will keep us together. My sisters and brothers, beware of the working power deep within because some of us need a helping hand. Having a strong impulse looming over the afflicted is a daunting task to take on. But, brothers and sisters, we need to have the wisdom and understanding to assist the afflicted over the horizon.

A gift of watering a seed has the same joy
as the one who receives the gift.

—1 Peter 4:10 (NIV)

Today I Was Found

A lot of God's children are in the awesome and active families. Most of us have just lost our connection to God. When we were out there going through our doom and gloom God saw and knew it would be beneficial to His lost children to start this family. Only God could have brought us together so we could share the love of God with those that don't know Him. Even those who had their doorknob or a chair as their God. Every now and then Jesus's name gets thrown in because of a spiritual awakening. Some of the family members are content with where they are. But most are taking the necessary steps to go higher with the power that has been given, to be led by the spirit, soul, and body. So we are called into action for love of all things in life. So we could live righteously with the other side of the family.

A good, good Father will find a way for His children to come back.

—Matthew 11:28 (NIV)

Today I Am

An idiot is an idiot, and a fool is a fool. But when understanding and wisdom is integrated into the action of an able body hopefully the idiot becomes a new creature that is respectable and introduced himself as a wise man. A foolish woman will be transformed into a woman who live by the words in Proverbs 31:10–31 (NIV). For the most part of our lives we did what we wanted to do. But now and forever the newness of life in a righteous way is a must. If all else fails, it would be a crying shame to be walking in the midst of wise idiots and fools.

How high is the bar set? When we say enough is really enough.

—2 Corinthians 12:20–21 (NIV)

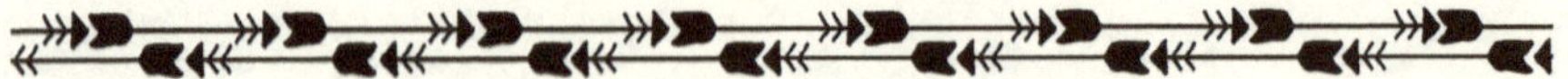

Again! Today

Never again! When we say never again. What are we truly saying to ourselves? By saying something or acting out of emotions in a moment of weakness or a lack of understanding, most of the time a mistake has occurred. In our lives that didn't pan out the way we wanted to. But it's a reason why we would say, "Never again." Again. It's because, when we are in a rush most decisions are made very quickly, and their maturity is little. But in the long run when we slow down the decisions we made. Some of them turn out to be gargantuan in statute that has us saying, "Never again." Never is not in our timeline. Life will never act in the same way, but it will show up again. In a way we may not recognize. But God will be there to show us that never saying "never" is a decision we had to make. So we can slow down in the midst of the rush hours of life.

Never again. Never again. But wisdom and
understanding will be there again and again.

—Romans 3:23 (KJV)

To Be Honest Today

Run after me, Father, as I seek your face. Don't allow me to let my hands go of yours, Lord Jesus. Don't stop counseling me, Holy Spirit, when I say something foolish. My pointed angels, don't leave me alone when I am in the midst of my own way.

Pure and honest from the heart. We can accomplish…

—2 Timothy 2:22 (NIV)

A Hold on to Today!

How much of a hold on today will God allow us to have? He knows what we do and say. The test of trials and tribulation we are going to go through. The pain and suffering our spirit, soul, and body it's going to endure. He knows all the people that are going to hurt us and who we are going to hurt. He also knows the joy and peace that we are going to have. The release from stress and fulfillment of overcoming a battle. The forgiving of trespasses to them and to ourselves. The love for ourselves and for others is going to become greater. How strong our faith is going to be in the day to come? The hurts, habits, hang-ups, triumphs, and victories are all for a hopeful future.

We can hold on for today but soon today will
release us into tomorrow forever and ever.

—Job 23 (NIV)

Today of All Hope

Today it shows up in a place that seems to be run down out of shape. It is safe to say that it's mind-blowing to find hope in a hopeless place. The biggest jaw-dropping experience about this hopelessness we go through is that majority of it is caused by our doubts. But the most mind-boggling is in the attitude of those who believed in God. The disregard of all that is being taught and abandoned all reason to join the world of enjoyment. Some will say that it is hopeless to have hope in a situation where it's beyond repair. We are not excluded from this hopelessness. It's just a matter of time. When the outbreak of confidence comes forth, the aggression of hopelessness transforms into the boldness of faith that all things are hopeful!

God has written the hopelessness in our story so others can
read about having faith in Him that they can overcome...

—Romans 8:28 (NIV)

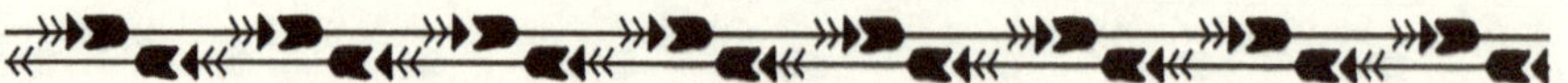

Today Just Be...

Being still takes a great deal of effort. But all heavenly things that are worth it can be had with time to seek it out. Then we all can dive right into the waters! Being still on our own can be achieved, and yet we can't hold a candle to the arrival when God is in attendance. Most people get lost in the timing. How long do I meditate? Five, ten, fifteen minutes—some can go a whole hour without falling asleep. As for myself (Cedric Easton) it took a while for me not to go to sleep. Now I slightly doze off, but I get up quickly. It's wonderful to let our thought process slow down so we can catch up to God and have some alone time.

Stillness is not a skill to have in life but it
is a requirement to live this life.

—Philippians 1:27–30 (NIV)

So Today Is A…

There was a point in my life when it was hard for me to get up and do the things I wanted in life. I know that I do have something to offer others. I just was tired of trying to grind it out. One day I talked to a therapist. She came up with something that will forever be with me. The ultimate encouragement for me to live by. She said, "Stop using the word *grind*, and use the word *goals*." And it hit me like a megaton of bricks! I don't have to grind because I've been grinding so hard to stay afloat. Also, I am allowing God to be the head of my day. I have learned a lot, and it's easy now to do move about my day without the stress of grinding it out.

God does not have to play with words in our lives. But He
does give the opportunities to play the words so we can
go through the day without grinding for our goals.

—Ecclesiastes 7:14 (NIV)

Today We Will…

Doing what we say and acting it out it's not easy. Even when we have put our mind to it. There is so much more that comes with it. That's a no-brainer of an answer to give. But when we grabbed hold of what we say and do to put it into the hands of God, all bets are off the table. What we say and do does have merit to those that are watching. Either to point us out on our garbage or to see if this God thing does work. When our actions lined up with the things of God we do have to think of what to say or do because it will be in front of us.

Our actions are what we hold dear to every fiber of
our being. And yet they are not without words of God
and the actions that Jesus took on the cross.

—1 John 3:19 (NIV)

I Got to Work Today!

Doing my due diligence. Back in the day I (Cedric Easton) used to get so upset when I was called to do something when I was in a group of people. In 2018, I was singled out to rake the yard at a facility I was staying in. I got upset. I did not use any obscene language, but I was pretty mad because no one else was appointed to this task with me. So, I put on my headphones, and I begin to listen to my music. I started to think about all the times this has happened to me, and it hit me. I have forgotten all that was taught to me about working for God and obedience is better than sacrifice. I started to laugh and began to enjoy the chore that was given to me.

When working unto God no matter what we are doing, work does seem so worky. Matter of fact sometimes, it turns into a celebration.

—Proverbs 12:24

Side note: When I was raking the yard I was listening to my gospel rap.

Today Studies

Studies show that if someone yells for help in a crowded place, most likely no one will come to help. But if they yell "Fire!" people come running into action. But an expert says if someone yells "Fire!" people would be terrified and run instead of be a hero. We have come to the point where people will not come to a person's aid in time. As God's children help always comes as needed according to the limit of our faith. So, next time when one of us is in a position to help out in a crowded place, allow the God in us to show and to show out.

Evil doesn't need help, but our enemies do.

—Romans 8:26 (NKJV)

Don't Let Today's Work Pass By

Providing aid to someone in their time of need does wonders for the heart and soul. We all have been selfish and done shameful things that have hardened us in ways where it is difficult to help another. But it's the limits to our heart where God wants us to let go of it. I (Cedric Easton) had such a moment. I couldn't quite understand why my foster mom kept asking me to do things around the house. It was getting to the point where my heart was at its limit. I got upset one day and said, "Why are you asking me to do these things when everyone else is here as well?" She tore me a new one. I didn't understand, even when she explained to me why always call me. Until one day that when I had done a good job on helping out or doing anything people always are going to ask for my help. It is one of the many gifts that God has given His children.

Go ahead and be the difference in someone's life. So
they can be different in somebody else's life.

—Colossians 3:23 (NKJV)

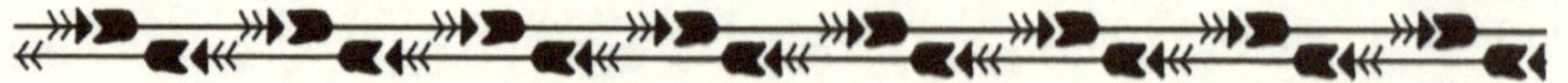

Today Starts a New Bloodline

Whose blood and who's not? We work so hard to have a belonging in life. We come to depend on the relationships we have in life. Even when they are falling apart or have been taken away by death or by imprisonment, we find it hard to let go. Most of the time we do not know how to cope with the emotions that come with it.

I became close with one of my pastors and his wife. That bond we share as we connected through our past made it even stronger. His wife and I when high-five one another at the same time we interlock our hands. Him and I became like brothers. Also became Uncle Ceddy. So one day pastor, his wife, another close friend of ours, and I were having a conversation. It got deep, and I said something about my past that they told me not to do, and I did it. They were furious, I just knew by their reactions that it was all over. But my pastor and his wife loved me like I was a real brother and they forgave me.

To live is to love. To laugh before we cry. As we say goodbye.

—Genesis 50:17 (NKJV)

P.S.: To my blood little brother. The blood is gone but the love is not.

Today's Winners Are!

Not just winning, we all know that being first in any sporting event is the reason why people train hard. But what if there's no placement at all. That wouldn't even beg the question. If there was no first-place reward., why do what they do if there were nothing to reach for? Would we have the same agenda in watching our favorite team play or track and field star? But there is a way to run a race or boxer fighting the good fight. Getting through hardship does not have any accolades to give out. But for, us as a child of God, it is the praise, glory, and honor to God. Having victory over hardship or a cry of triumph through a stronghold holds no first-place winner. To smile with a sigh of relief and joy within the heart. The only loss in life is a loved one running or fighting without the biggest supporter it gets even harder to live.

We run, jump, throw, swim, and fight as hard as we can so
the ones we've lost can live on in love and in our dreams.

—2 Timothy 4:7 (NKJV)

Today We Look Back

The day that passed. Looking into the past is not profitable to anyone if they are not learning from it to move forward. Doing something new that's going to alter our lives. It requires change with the mind, growth in faith, and a will that bends but does not break. We cannot fulfill our future without strengthening the day that we are in now. Evil loves to go back to the day of our past when we were doing wrong. But our past is full of good, bad, and the ugly. Our past is in between God and evil. We can do our best to leave it behind and yet we take it to every new place we go.

Mistakes are in the past and also in the days to come.

—1 Peter 4:3 (NKJV)

Today I Spent

Our pastime is for us to enjoy, but when it's going to help some-one in their time of need then it becomes a whole different type of spending our pastime. In the name of Jesus! I (Cedric Easton) enjoy my pastime in God's words because it helps me as much as it will help others. I've spent so much time doing self things. Even when I wasn't out there in my doom and gloom. It used to mess with me so much that I could not stop thinking about it and self-consciously could not let it go. But in the Bible study my pastor and one of the sisters told me not to worry about it because she hasn't been a pastor, and the sister didn't believe for years. After that mind-blowing fact my thinking quickly changed. Now my day is spent in a way that shows up in God's way.

Moments are counted by the day-to-day actions that do
not stray from the directions that God has put forth.

—Galatians 5:16–24 (NKJV)

Today I...

Catch and release. We are in this world but not of it so we should not be all up in arms about letting go of something we've worked so hard for. Even when we've done something to have it being released from our possession. When I (Cedric Easton) was dismissed from the Salvation Army with a little over twenty people for company purposes, I went home and cried because it was my fault that they let me go. It was not in the will of God. It was of this world, and I got into a car crash.

My left shoulder had some damage, and they couldn't keep me on the job. Even though I was one of their best workers. Weeks later I am mailing out the last of the rent and saw my roommate outside of the job. So I rode my bike to him, but I had to ride fast to catch up to him before he went in. As he saw me, he told me to go inside, get some air for my back tire, and talk to the boss about getting my job back. By this time my shoulder had a doctor's note to come back to work, and I got my job back. Within those past few weeks my faith in God grew. I wasn't worried about the things I had, and He gave me more than I had before.

The moment in life when letting go and
allow God to let life run its course.

—1 Thessalonians 5:18 (NKJV)

Today I Create A Place

To be at ease... Relaxed... On a day at its rockiest, the emotions of a beautiful sunset can be blocked out in the corners of the mind. God had sent His son to us out of love. To teach and show us how to live a life like Him and to do greater things than Him. The things that Jesus went through in the eyes of heaven and in front of men. It was not impressive. It was spiritually mind-dusting and the four winds of the earths blow them into another atmosphere never to be seen again. The people that saw this did not have a good day, and if we were there, our lives would have been shipwrecked as well. Even before a drop of blood poured out, Jesus had entered into a place where the pure spot in His mind and stayed there. What we go through on a daily basis even on the other side of the earth Jesus has prepared a place where the mind can go in the midst of the body going through trauma. The presence of the Holy Spirit is the most rewarding gift in life.

Creating a place in the mind with God is the best place to relax.

—Ephesians 4:23 (NIV)

Picture the Movements
of Today

As the morning moves along with the action of righteousness. As the morning step gently it comes ever so closely to the afternoon. As the day arms open wide to embrace the afternoon. And as the day cultivates the time when the sky changes colors. As the evening arrives a canvas of the sky activates a sunset. The colors are mixed with a light blue, shade of misty orange, and dancing with a pink silver lining. Swirling together with a relaxing background of clouds. Now that the night has ushered the stars into place and all its brilliance, let us not forget what we went through and the sight that we've seen. Something that we will never see again! When God gives us days and moments like this then we can truly take advantage of the days and moments like this.

When evil likes to throw monkey wrenches in our garage
do forget that there is a place to put those kinds of tools.

—James 1:16–17 (NIV)

Today I Say

Say it to me. So I can say it to others. The things that have been said within the most inner part of our hearts. It comes from God in the place where wisdom and understanding of who we are in Christ Jesus. Where we should dwell but at times we do lose sight of what we say. When the emotions come bubbling up allowing the words to others or ourselves, contradicting our actions and beliefs in the eyes of man. The things we say to others have to be kept in the healthy hands of God. We all know that things can get out of hand when our flesh wants to arise. That's why the spirit is first, second comes the soul, and last the flesh. We have to operate in that order. When the actions of what's behind others to get us out of character. A pastor once said, "Do not get mad at the person but get mad the evil that's behind them."

The word of love is written into the fleshly heart.

—Proverbs 16:24 (NIV)

Today I Am!

I would rather be a snowball thrown out of Jesus's hands than a playful child. I would rather be the snow that has not yet fallen than the snow on a majestic mountain. I would rather be the flower that is not yet seen by nature's own eye. I would rather be the dirt under Jesus's feet than be welcome at the table of rich men. I would rather be shattered in the hands of the Father than broken in this world. I would rather be what God wants me to be than just being me.

When we were living in this world it was just
what it was nothing more nothing less.

—Proverbs 17:21 or Galatians 3:26

Today's Time Is It?

Today time will be well-spent. It is the time that we will spend most in our lives with God and others. Whatever we do and where we go time is winding down, but it's also being added to the days to come. We have to understand that the time we take from God and others has to be cherished, so it will become the time that has not been squandered, and we have built a shell of a house to leave behind.

Everything gets old in time, but the moments
will be renewed at the end.

—Hebrews 3:13 (NIV)

What Have I Learned Today?

The day that I understood. The day of knowing that everything is going to be okay and of those to come. To have that feeling of knowing that in the midst of it all. Truly believing wholeheartedly in the peace that passes all understanding. And of the things God is doing in my life. To live like this is the moment that is beyond my fleshly desires. So when things are not going the way I think they should, I have to sit back, relax, and remember that God's desires will become my own. To allow Jesus to run loose in the movements of my day.

It will be a shame to let the day ticktock
away without the Holy Spirit.

—Colossians 1:9 (NIV)

The Great, Greater, and Greatest of Today!

Being part of an awesome and active family is experiencing newness in life, but there's a downside to it. Like we don't have much room to slack off. Soon as we relax in well-doing and just let go of the hard work we put in on being sober-minded. We will miss out on being *great* in all we can do. We definitely won't recognize that the *greater* that's is in that wants us to be great and to go beyond. So we have to do our best to stay *close* to the ones who got us this far and stay *closer* to God so we can become the *closest* to beginning the *greatest* we can be in this life and beyond. We know how *easy* it is to just fall off the map and don't want to be seen by people. But we also know that it gets *easier* the more work we put in to stay in the eyes of God. So the *easiest* way out is going to be *hard*, and the *harder* we work on it will be the *hardest* thing we do in life.

Putting the *good* away allows the *better* to be had. But leaving
all that behind gives us a chance for the *greatest* of them all.

—Galatians 6:9 (NIV)

How many groups are in sequence?

Today Can't Be Wasted

When the mind is wasted it is shrouded in darkness. Let's take myself (Cedric Eastin) for example. I knew once I had made up my mind that I was going out to drink. Even though I knew what the consequence of all my actions would be. My pastor and his wife knew that once my mind had that thought I was a goner. My mind was drowning in sorrow and high on despair; it took a lot away from me. My thought process was shut, but God knew where I needed to be. I got help from a place where God developed a new mindset in me. In church, Bible study, or discussions. It is read in 2 Timothy 2:25 (KJV). Reading God's word allowed me to keep my mind from going off the deep end. I hated my mind for many different reasons, but a lovely lady told me that my mind is a gift.

> The mind jumps through so many loopholes. That's probably the reason why we can use its full potential.

> —2 Peter 3:15

P.S.: Filling my thoughts with God's words weighed my head down. Now I can say I got something heavy on my mind.

Today Heard Them Say…

Listening is one of the wisest acts that the body does. When we open ourselves to others to hear them out it's a connection far beyond what we truly realize. There are two things that I (Cedric Easton) do when I'm listening. I like to make eye contact, and this second one may sound weird, but I look at the mouth so I can picture the words coming out. Those two acts help me focus on what the person is saying.

One thing that I heard from a pastor is that when the opportunity occurs, I say a small quick prayer as I listen. So I can give what needs to be given from God and not myself. But the best things happen when listening. Some may cry, laugh, or smile, but there is one that dominates them all—it is when the person leaves with the world, lifted off of them. God has given all of us the act of listening well. but He has given some the gift of listening.

Laughing under the influence keeps the pain away
for a moment, but smiling with peace of mind
influences others to laugh their pain away freely.

—Philippians 2:4 (NKJV)

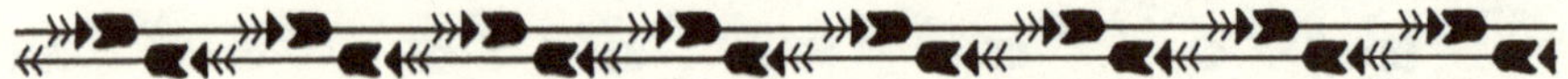

Today's Reality

There is no such thing as a false feeling. But when we are not true to our feelings a false sense of reality comes out as a smile, and some have perfected the method of a fake smile. I (Cedric Easton) had the opportunity to have my smile wiped away by God and have Him give me His smile. I had been prophesied over many times, but there was one that really stuck with me.

This lady was kind of a nonsense type of person as far as I could tell. So one Sunday the leaders of the church (LHFC) lined up in front and the whole congregation went through. Everybody spoke encouraging words from the start all the way until the end. This lady told me, "God is not impressed with the laughing and the joking." I was really down and out because I was taking my program really seriously. I was doing everything unto God. So I asked God to reveal it to me. See my joy was not real for a long time, and I knew it deep inside of me. I released all of my feelings unto God and since then my days are at ease.

A smile installed by God. It warms the bones, takes a stab at
evil, drowns out the sorrow, and it brings joy to others.

—Numbers 6:24–26 (NKJV)

Can I Relax Today?

As the chest inhales, hold it for one, two, and three exhales. Now with closed eyes, take in one more deep breath, but this time clear the mind, relax the shoulders, feel the chest expanding as the air is introduced to the lungs, and feel the chest contract as the air is being released. Okay, let's go all together! Breath in. Hold it. One, two, three. And breath out.

The moment has come. When everything is joined together, twisted beyond recognition, and contorted in ways that boggle the mind. A sign of relief is in order. Some would say that a child of God should not be stressed out, and they are true. But when we are in tune with God our stress level does not disappear. It gets lower, the mind isn't so worn out, the shoulders are relaxed, and the chest isn't so tight. When we ask Jesus to calm the storm in us let's not forget that God will not give us more than we can handle it.

Stressing out without release is taking the power away from God.

—Exodus 14:14 (NKJV)

Today!

What beautiful things that God had created for us to see today! When we get that chance to see the things that are prepared by the hands of the Father! To identify these things and to capture the moments in our lives. They are not rare; they are not some mystical creature trying to be elusive. To experience a place that we have not seen is something to hold and treasure for life. But when the sight beholds something marvelous in the backyard it's God's way of telling us that we are at the right place and right timing. So stay tuned in the life's channel because the eyes will see the oohs and aahs in all its splendor that one director can create.

What can be seen will not always be understood, but what we don't see will be known by the understanding of the Holy Spirit behind.

—Hebrews 2:4 (NKJV)

The Simplest Things for Today!

It's a rare moment when a member of the church says something that catches the pastor off guard. One of my pastors was giving a sermon about how he puts on the armor of God before leaving the house. And one of the sisters said, "Why take it off? I keep mine on all the time." The pastor was taken back because he had never thought of it like that. So now that is what he preaches every time he talks about the armor of God. When someone simplifies something for us that is so godly, it blows our mind. That we just can't keep holding on for a rainy day. I (Cedric Easton) can imagine the revelations my pastor got from that outburst of wisdom.

The joy of simplifying something that's so simple.

—Ecclesiastes 7:29 (NIV or GNT)

When the Day Is…

When a heart is so heavy that it weighs down the spirit. When it can't form the words to cry out unto God. This is a heart that many of us have carried around before. It's hard to live life as a child of God in that manner. To be in a church setting in the back hoping no one comes and starts the talk. Because then the heaviness gets exposed, and it's a whole issue that obviously needs to be addressed. But a lot of people don't want that even in the church. For some odd reason some of us fail to realize that when Jesus was in the garden His heart was so heavy that He was sweating enormous drops of blood. We don't have to lean on one side when we walk because our heart is that heavy.

The heaviness of life is no joke, and the
heaviness of God is no joke either.

—Philippians 4:1–7

The Newness of Today

When the loudness of this world gets unbearable the cries of our hearts are being heard by the Father. The first time when we were young, not of age but in the heart when we came to God. Not knowing how to truly pray when we are at odds with the things of this world and not knowing how or when it's the right time to talk it out with a sister or a brother and ask for guidance. I (Cedric Easton) know it was hard for me, from the end of 2018 all the way to the middle of 2019. Everything started to happen for me because I truly understood that my timing does not matter. My prayers became more powerful and effective. The peace that has been given unto me along with the smile God planted on my face. I don't do my best to give it to others. It just automatically comes out of me and infects the atmosphere. I just hope that I can put a smile on God's face at the end.

No matter the age we are, we are still young in Christ Jesus.

—1 Corinthians 13:11 (NKJV)

Today Is Just...

The moment when the rain starts to let up and the sky releases the sun. The clouds say, "It's okay for us to come out and give God's children some shade." We can act way outside the box on days like this. A time to breath and relax, a time to play and rejoice, to have that time to just slide down life's longest slide and land on fluffy clouds. As the rocking chair goes back and forward, as the hammock hangs in balance, and as the floating bed suspends outside in the breeze. No matter how we spend this day we can honestly say, "This is the day that the Lord has made."

Sometimes the flesh does like to enjoy what God is doing.

—Philippians 4:4–9 (NIV)

Through Today's Storm

To give the storm a high five. When the sun is trying to gaze through the gray clouds. The rain has calmed down to a slight drizzle, and the wind went from a roaring lion to a breathing baby. The heaviest part of the storm has passed; the streets may be flooded but not the house. Thank God! Praying for those that are not faring well in their storm. As the night falls it continues to drizzle, but the stars are out, and it's looking nice. Tomorrow is going to be a good day but as of tonight sound mind and sound body as the occupants sleep on this firm foundation. In Jesus's name amen.

To be proud of the storm that I am in is to
rejoice when I get to cut the grass.

—Acts 27:18–26 (NIV)

The Effect that Today Has

How great it is to wake up with the clouds? How sweet is it to be the morning dew? How lovely would it be to become the horizon with the precious creatures of the sky? To ride along with the kindness of the wind. Mesmerized while soaring of life that lives on and on. Going in and out, moving around from cloud to cloud. The sun lights shining from side to side. Something so beautiful, something so wonderful, and something so powerful. The sky is woven together for life to be lived in the tapestry from the designer, the King I'm so aware of. Somewhere the sounds of *drip drop drip drop* splash after splash long and short. From point to point the steps of nature. It started here and ended there with a rainbow on a canvas that is painted. For a sight to hold and never like it to be seen again.

To be part of something that will have a lasting effect on someone or in something can only be given by God.

—Psalm 145:5 (NIV)

The Power of Today!

The power of life is that act to live. The difference between experience and awoke. To have seen it and lived it. To allow someone to help us go further than the twelve steps of life. With the step by step guidance as Jesus walks beside His co-heirs. The true gift of life starts with Jesus. He keeps going on with the soberness of life. A promise is fulfilled in love and by its action. The design of life is rough, but the blessings are at every stop along the road of life that will be addressed. Life is good no matter how the eyes see. The pages we all know are written and the Book of Life, so let's work on living freely. Let's not just talk about it but let salvation be the voice of our actions.

The greatness of life should not be after its end and yet it is.

—John 6:36 (NIV)

The Weak of Today

The weakness of the flesh is something. The moment when we feel so strong in our faith that we can lift up a mountain and throw it into the sea on another planet. And yet we are so fragile like fine china inside of a blender being disintegrate, and thrown into a hurricane and dropped off into the deepest part of the sea. Some of us do come back to the seashore like a message in a bottle. It's wonderful to feel someone touching the glass and to put the top off and read all that we've gone through. To be strong against the flesh is a battle not easily won.

The longer war goes on the longer it takes
for the spirit and soul to heal.

—Galatians 5:16 (NKJV)

Start Today

Why not when the fact is that it will help? A lot of my active and awesome family members don't want to hear about the total spiritual life. What's wrong with the spiritual action that gets lives out of darkness and into the light? A lot of my family members blame God for what they went through. Not knowing that God does not interfere with free will. They have made promises to God not knowing that His words are the law. That He will fulfill His that He made to us not the other way around. But some of us do get the changes to say things about prayer, Jesus, and the Holy Spirit. Just to let them know and see. How is our power?

> Let's not allow the opportunity to pass us by. When
> we have the golden moment to put Jesus's name into
> a place where God's name has been spoken.

—Psalm 113:3 (NKJV)

Boxing the Day

Things that don't look right together. Like wearing a plaid jacket and striped pants. Wearing a wedding dress with jean pants under it. Like getting dressed in the dark as the task is done a thought comes across the mind. Let's look at everything really quick so a glance is taken in the mirror. Shirt, shorts, and shoes. Looking good. Got the keys. Let's go. As morning rolls along some point out the mix matched sock. It was done on purpose, but nonetheless it had happened. We don't always do things on purpose but do to get attention or just do really do care. There is one thing that we have done on purpose but not meaning to—it's putting God in a box.

Putting restrictions on God is like wrapping the lips
around a straw to draw a breath and sneeze. Better yet
it's like breathing underwater with a coffee straw.

—Ephesians 3:20 (NKJV)

Ask for It

We all know that it's hard for men to ask for help. When it comes to the BBQ on the grill, fixing something, or the age-old asking for directions. We all know that women are highly strong with their emotions. They don't drive very well, they shop a lot, and they overreact. No matter how we see that there is a well-known struggle that plagues women and men. It's not embedded in our DNA that the majority of men on this earth are like what is described, and that goes the same for women. Asking for help is not embarrassing, but being prideful is. Hitting rock bottom is not a struggle, but reaching for the top without reaching for help is a struggle all of its own.

People say acceptance is half the battle. If that
is true, what is at the start of the battle?

—Hebrews 4:16 (NKJV)

Don't Drown Today

When we lose focus, everything suffers. I (Cedric Easton) belong to two families that are working toward the same end to live a righteous life. The first family I was adapted to is the church. We can't lose sight of what God has for us and what He has done. To love God with all of our being and to love others as we love ourselves. The other family I gravitated toward is my awesome and active family. If we lose focus, all is forgotten, and life will cease to exist. To be sober mind is what we live for in a way. Only God can do for us what we could not do for ourselves. To not lose focus is to renew the mind daily. So we can remind ourselves who we are unto God and what we have to do.

> Suffering is going to happen but staying
> vigilant is key while suffering.

—Philippians 3:14 (NKJV)

Today Has a Love

The same type of love from the smallest of hugs to a bear hug. To the unknowing love that's behind the scenes or the right in the face kind of love. The love that suffered on the cross so we can suffer less within our hearts. The love that shines throughout the world is the same love that shields us from it. This love does not boast, but it does get a boost. There's no ugly side of love only in the hearts that have no use for it. Love is not on this earth to take a side, but it is on every side it can take.

Love has no face, but we can picture it on every person we see.

—1 Corinthians 13 (NKJV)

The Spoken Truth for Today

Speaking the truth has two different facts. The first one is full of joy, happiness, kindness, love, and all the things that God offered to us. That is the truth that a lot of people want to hear. Who does not want to hear some words that lift the spirit and leave with a smile on the face? The second part of truth is speaking that comes with but is attached to it. With pain, suffering, and sometimes feeling that life is not worth living. But that unworthy part is just in our heads. God did not make a worthless life, yet there is something, and that the Seeker will lift us up in a way that we cannot hold on to. A lot of people want to hear a happy feel-good message that tickles the ear. But most of us want a word from God—that message that lifts us up in a way it makes us feel good but gives us that old-school sixties batman. The pow! The bam! The biff! The whamm!

A truthful word that is painful gives a shine to life. Mean
it when it's said. Just don't be mean while saying it.

—John 16:13 (NKJV)

Thanks for Today

Today is one of those days, and yet the day is not like those days. We have said that line sometimes that we forget that God did not make today like one of those days. We should love the fact that God made it that way I (Cedric Easton) am glad that my past days are not like my upcoming days. All that I went through is not something I want my feelings today to be. So I'm embracing the so-called one of those kinds of days. I love you, my Father, who is in heaven. Thank you, Jesus, for bridging the gap, and the Holy Spirit, thank you for the inspiration.

Today is the day I let today be its own.

—Ephesians 5:20 (NKJV)

About the Author

Cedric Easton's passion to be a writer began in the ninth grade as a result of assistance and encouragement from his English teacher. However, he has fought numerous battles throughout his lifetime. He has overcome dyslexia, bouncing from one foster home to the next from the age of four to eighteen, alcoholism, drug addiction, and homelessness. Despite these hurdles, Cedric's dreams, including being a writer, persevered. He attributes his success to God's strength and guidance and people whom God placed along the way, consisting of guidance counselors, job coaches, a foster mom in high school, members of his church, family members, etc.

Places that have particularly helped him are the Lighthouse in Riverview, Florida, and the Rope Center in Hudson, Florida. Another dream, to be a husband and a father, has also come to fruition. Originally from Sarasota, Florida, where he lived for most of his childhood, Cedric now lives with his wife and son in the Tampa Bay area of Florida. He hopes his writing will inspire all of God's children to be more unified and connected with the words God has given us.